T0380631

# THE PLAN

THE PLAN

# THE PLAN

CARLOS H. VASQUEZ

Archway Publishing books may be ordered through booksellers or by contacting:

Archway Publishing
1663 Liberty Drive
Bloomington, IN 47403
www.archwaypublishing.com
844-669-3957

Because of the dynamic nature of the Internet, any web addresses or links contained in this book may have changed since publication and may no longer be valid. The views expressed in this work are solely those of the author and do not necessarily reflect the views of the publisher, and the publisher hereby disclaims any responsibility for them.

Any people depicted in stock imagery provided by Getty Images are models, and such images are being used for illustrative purposes only. Certain stock imagery © Getty Images.

ISBN: 978-1-6657-5659-4 (sc)
ISBN: 978-1-6657-5660-0 (e)

Library of Congress Control Number: 2024902819

Print information available on the last page.

Archway Publishing rev. date: 03/05/2024

# About the Author

Despite Carlos H. Vasquez growing up in very humble beginnings from Spanish Harlem to the Lower East Side in New York City, his education has spanned from coast to coast and even study abroad.

He is a proud graduate of Pace University and New York City Community College in New York City, as well as, Los Angeles Valley College in California. He has also pursued Paralegal Studies at the University of West Los Angeles and French at the University of Laval in Quebec City Canada.

He has been an Investigator for the Department of Homeless Services in New York City, Chief of the Process Serving Unit at the New York Law Department, as well as, in charge of Security for the dormitories of the University of Southern California. He has also received acknowledgments for the Security of the 1984 Olympic Games, as well as, the Rodney King Civil Disturbance in Los Angeles in 1992.

He is presently the author of the novel "The Adventures of Gabriel" and lives in California.

# Dedication

This book is dedicated to my whole family. My brother and sisters, cousins, nieces and nephews, and grand nieces and nephews, as well as my little neighbors Luna and JoJo who are growing up in an era where companies and banks are pushing credit cards, but not telling them what to do when the bill comes due.

As kids we were told to "Save for a rainy day". With global warming and lack of empathy for your fellow man it seems those days are coming more frequently today than ever before.

This Plan is your umbrella.

# Introduction

As I write this book someone has won a 1.3 billion dollar Mega. The Power ball is up to 187 million dollars, and the Super lotto is at 12 million dollars.

Most of us can only dream of what we would do if we got that kind of money. We live paycheck to paycheck, we're deep in debt or worst we're homeless. The reality is that we are where we are because most of us do not have a "Plan".

And, the other reality is that if you can't manage a $12 an hour job, you will not get a sudden burst of wisdom if you wake up tomorrow and realize you have a 1.3 billion dollar ticket burning your pocket. Within five or ten years you will be right back where you are right now.

So, the trick is to learn how to manage money when you have very little of it or, none at all. Because, when you hit the Lottery, it is then too late to learn.

I do not pretend to know everything. After all, I just bought my Lottery tickets. But, I have done more with a $10 an hour job than many people have done with five times that much.

I was born in dire poverty and grew up in a broken, but loving home, in tenement buildings and a housing project. Yet, I have several college degrees, I speak seven languages and I have partied in Paris, London, Rome and Venice.

I have been inside the Vatican and the Roman Coliseum. I have taken pictures in front of The Leaning Tower of Pisa, The Eiffel Tower, Buckingham Palace, and the site of the 1976 Winter Olympics in Innsbruck, Austria.

And, I have done all this making less than $12 an hour.

I have written this book in the hope that I can help someone reach even higher aspirations than I did, no matter where they are financially right now.

CARLOS H. VASQUEZ

# Homelessness

Let me start with Homelessness.

For six years I investigated homeless families in New York City. I interviewed homeless people, their families and friends.

I interviewed in person or on the phone more than 12 people a day for six years.

I interviewed in the office, in tenement buildings, in Housing Projects and Luxury homes.

I interviewed people all over New York City, in different states and in different countries.

I too came to this job with many misconceptions and left with a wealth of wisdom. Among the most prominent misconception was that "mental illness causes homelessness". I found the opposite, that "homelessness caused mental illness". The longer people remained homeless the less control of their lives they felt.

More than half the people I interviewed had jobs, but could not afford rising rents.

What was common among most of them was that they didn't have a "Plan".

That is why I am writing this book. In the hope of giving everyone a Plan.

If you are homeless and reading this book, do not believe for a second that you can not regain control over your life again. If you can read this book, then you are halfway there.

I leave you with one thought:

What is the difference between a "Rich Person" and a "Wealthy Person"?

Answer:

A "Rich Person" knows how to make money.

A "Wealthy Person" knows how to keep it.

# So Here is the Plan

1) **First:**

A "Plan" begins with a re-evaluation of where you are right now.

2) **Second:**

You must figure out where you want to go.

3) **Third:**

And, this is the most important part, you must put those two things together by reflecting on the vehicle that will take you there.

The first step is to get a job, any job. I don't care how much it pays as long as the pay is consistent and predictable.

Second, if you have a choice, ask for direct deposit into your Savings Account.

If you ask people to "save", their brain registers this function as "a sacrifice". Therefore, they come up with reasons why they cannot learn to sacrifice. They are just not willing to learn.

But, most people have no problem spending.

You have money, you see something and you buy it. It doesn't matter if you need it. It just matters that you want it.

Spending makes people feel secure. It makes people feel in control of their lives.

I am always fascinated by people who say that they have trouble putting $25 into their Savings Account every month, but religiously pay $700 a month for five years for a car payment without missing a beat.

So, if you have no trouble "Spending", but have trouble "Saving", have your whole check go into your "Savings Account". You have now learned to save. Now all you have to learn is how to "Spend".

# Spending

Learning how to spend becomes real easy once you know how much money comes in and how much goes out.

You would be surprised at how many people do not know that.

There are people who make massive amounts of money, but only realize how much money they made after they've spent it all.

Let's start with some basic understandings:

# Credit Cards

**First**, Credit Card money is not your money!

Credit Card money belongs to the Credit Card Company. You are only borrowing it.

And worst, you have to pay it back with interest.

**Second,** having a Credit Card limit does not mean you make more money.

If you make $30,000 a year and you have a $5,000 Credit Card limit it does not mean that you make $35,000 a year.

In fact, it usually means that you only make $27,000 a year because the other $3,000 went on interest.

**Third,** most of the things you buy with a Credit Card are not emergencies. So, don't use that as an excuse to take money out of your Savings Account to pay it back.

Once you pay off the Credit Cards you have now, put them away and never take them out unless you have a real emergency.

Getting a 50 inch T.V. or the latest I-Phone is not a real emergency. If you can't pay it with your Debit Card you can't afford it.

# Beware of the Words "Cash Back"

Every day we watch our favorite actors on T.V. say things like:

"I work hard for my money, and I want my money to work hard for me."

And then, they use the words: "Cash Back".

Don't be fooled by those words. Do the Math:

If you spend $10,000. Multiply that by 1% and see what you get back. You get back $100.

If they are charging you 29% on your Credit Card you are paying them $2,900 in interest.

Nobody is giving you anything back.

If you want to get anything back, then from your next paycheck take $100 and put it in your Savings Account.

You may get very little back in interest, but at least you are accomplishing more than with your Credit Card.

At least you are truly getting Cash Back.

# Why Inflation Exists

The number one question I used to get as a Real Estate agent was:

"How much is my house worth?"

My answer:

"What ever someone is willing to pay for it."

If I am selling a pen I bought for one dollar to someone willing to pay ten dollars for it, then that pen is worth ten dollars.

If I can get you to buy a $4,000 car for $20,000 by telling you that you will only have to pay $250 a month, then there is no incentive for me to lower the price of the car to $4,000 or even $10,000.

The more you buy things with a Credit Card the higher the price will remain.

To you it will appear as "Affordable".

### Businesses are no longer competing for your money.

Businesses are competing for your attention. They know that once they have your attention, your Credit Card money will flow easily to them with very little consideration or thought by you.

They are getting their money upfront, while you are the one stuck with the bill.

# Bills

Now that you have money in your Savings, the question is: How much money will I have to transfer from my Savings to my Checking in order to pay my bills?

In order to know this you have to know what type of bills you have, and what is the sum of those bills.

# There are two kinds of bills: Permanent and Flexible.

**Permanent bills are:**

Rent
Mortgage
Gas
Electricity
Water

And sometimes:
Car Insurance

**Flexible bills are:**

Credit Cards
Food
Clothes
Incidentals (Toilet paper, Woman's products, etc.)

# Definitions

**Permanent bills** are bills that you have to pay every month no matter how much money you make.

Even if you paid off your house, you will still have to pay Taxes, Insurance, Electricity, Gas and Water.

List these bills, estimating the ones that vary by usage.

Now take the sum of all of these bills and write the Sum down.

**Flexible bills** are the ones you have more control over.

You can spend more in one area today, and less in that area tomorrow.

With these bills you can delay having something this month, and instead chose to buy it next month.

When you have extra money you can increase your Credit Card payments and pay them off quicker, giving you even more extra money.

Estimate the amount of money you spend in each of these areas.

Now take the Sum of all of these areas and write the number down.

# Add both Sums

Add the sums of both the Permanent bills and the Flexible bills.

**Permanent bills + Flexible bills =**

If this total comes out higher than the amount of money coming into your household then you are living beyond your means.

Check to see if there is something in the Flexible bills that you can spend a little less on.

This total of Permanent and Flexible bills should not exceed more than 70% of your monthly take home income after taxes. If it does, cut down on something.

**This is the way I do it:**

I do it by bringing my lunch to work rather than eating at a restaurant or Starbucks everyday.

Another way I do it is when I go shopping for food.

I have found that some of the foods that I buy frequently are marked down on certain days. I stock up and save a bundle.

However, be careful. Make sure you buy only what you are going to eat. Throwing away food, is throwing away money.

Every day I thank God for the 99 cent Store. I shop there first. If I can't find it there I go to the regular supermarket.

I find everything from toothpaste and bandages to dish washing liquid and detergent. There are also food items and school supplies that I get cheaper than the regular supermarket.

Since I make my own coffee for work, I usually shop for it at the 99 cent store or Costco.

Since I am single, the rotisserie chicken at Costco gives me lots of options, from sandwiches to soups.

# Clothes and Electronics

Clothes and electronics are another area to save if you know what stores and when they offer the sales.

However, be careful about this area. If you don't need it, don't buy it.

Also remember this: Printers are very cheap. The companies are practically giving them away. But, they get their money back when you have to buy the ink.

Try whole sale ink places online that offer big discounts.

I would like to remind you again. Shop for all of this with your Debit Card, NOT your Credit Card. If you don't have enough money in your Checking and you need it, buy it later.

Remember, a car breakdown is an emergency. The latest I-Phone is not.

**Now let's talk about those Credit Cards.**

# Credit Cards

I don't care whether it's rent, Credit Cards or Cable T.V. When somebody tells you that that is the going "Rate", what they really mean is: "Everybody else is ripping you off. And, we want to rip you off too."

Today businesses can go into an app and learn what the latest "Rip Off" rate is and that is what they want to charge you.

Today we don't have Monopolies. We have Oligopolies.

So, when you have Credit Cards part of your "Plan" should always be to pay them off in full and not use them, except in dire emergencies, such as a car breakdown.

You should never have more than two Cards; one Debit and one Credit. Anything more than that means you are pretending to be richer than you really are.

Also, remember that if a store is offering you an item that costs $2,500 for $30 a month you are not paying $2,500 for it.

Chances are that you are paying a lot more for it because you are financing it. By the time you pay it off, it will be time to get a new one. That is what the businesses are counting on.

# So, now we come to the "Plan" to pay them off.

1) **First,** gather all your credit cards and list them in order from highest to lowest interest Rate. Write down how much you owe in each.

Interest Rates are where Card companies make their money. That is why if you pay the minimum payment only, your balance will only go down a tiny amount.

Your new balance will be made up of your old balance plus more Interest.

Beware that some Credit Card Companies will charge you two interest rates at the same time. One for a purchase you made last year and another for a purchase you made last week.

They will not tell you this. They will simply apply your payments to one purchase, allowing the other to grow your balance.

2) **Second,** Try to pay more than the minimum payment on all the Cards. However, pay the highest amount on the Card with the highest Interest.

If the amount on one of the Cards is a small enough amount, pay it off in full. This will then free you of that Credit Card payment and give you more money to pay off the others.

Once you have paid them off, stay with the Card which is most Universal and has the lowest interest rate. If you buy something with this Card pay it off immediately if possible.

**Remember**: Minimum payments prolong the pain.

**Keep this also in mind:**

Stores will offer you their Credit Cards. The trouble with these Cards is that you will think that you are getting such a great deal that you will continue to buy things you don't need.

The bills from multiple Cards will get higher and higher until you find yourself in a financial hole.

# A way to pay off credit cards

**First:**

Create four columns;

1) Name of Credit Card

2) Amount you owe

3) Interest rate of the card

4) Minimum payment for that card

**Second:**

Place the columns horizontally;

| Name of card | Amount owed | Interest rate | Minimum payment |
|---|---|---|---|
| a) Capital One | $7,539.27 | 29% | $150.00 |
| b) Chase | $6,046.32 | 28% | $100.00 |
| c) Macy's | $2,053.12 | 22% | $60.00 |
| d) Discover | $1,302.96 | 29% | $50.00 |

Make sure you list the cards from the highest amount owed to the lowest.

CARLOS H. VASQUEZ

**Third:**

Disregard the thousands column on the amount you owe.

**Fourth:**

Look at the five numbers of the amount you owe.

**Fifth:**

If the amount is less than the minimum payment, add that amount to the minimum payment, and pay that amount as your payment for that month.

**Sixth:**

If the last five numbers on the amount you owe is greater than the minimum payment, pay that instead of the minimum amount.

**Note:**

If this is too hard financially, follow this procedure with the last four numbers rather than the last five numbers.

**Another way is to combine the two:**

a) Follow the procedure using the last five numbers for the card you owe the most, or the card you owe the least.

b) Then follow the four number procedure for the other cards.

You can also follow the five number procedure with the card with the highest interest rate. And, follow the four number procedure with the rest.

**Note:**

When the amount you owe drops below $500, try to pay it off completely. This will free you from one of the cards and put more money into the Plan.

**Remember:**

The objective is to get rid of "ALL" your credit cards.

The secret to Long Life, is Short Debt!

# Now Let's Review

1) You took stock of where you are right now, and where you want to be next year.

2) You got a job. Remember, any job. As long as the pay is consistent and predictable.

3) You asked to be paid by Direct Deposit. (If you don't have a bank account, I am assuming that you will open one).

You want this Deposit to be into your Savings Account.

If you split it between the Savings and the Checking, the amount that goes into the Checking should never change. The rest should go to Savings.

Remember, you are learning to "Spend". The Savings will take care of itself.

4) You have split your bills into Permanent and Flexible bills.

You have compared this to your income. Adjusting where necessary in order to get the Spending below 70% of your monthly take home pay after taxes.

5) You've learned to Spend by saving money.

You go to the discount stores and shop in the supermarkets on mark down days.

You only shop for what you need. Remember, throwing away food, is throwing away money.

6) You've learned that Credit Card money is not your money.

Credit Cards do not make you richer, they make you poorer.

Now the only thing we haven't talked about is "Overtime". So, let's do that now.

# Overtime

Overtime is extra money to which you are entitled. It comes in many forms.

A) Some come as Paid Holidays.

| | |
|---|---|
| 1) New Year's Day | January 1$^{st}$. |
| 2) Memorial Day | Last Monday in May |
| 3) Independence Day | July 4$^{th}$ |
| 4) Labor Day | First Monday in September |
| 5) Thanksgiving | Fourth Thursday in November |
| 6) Christmas Day | December 25$^{th}$ |

B) Other Overtime comes when another employee doesn't show up to work and you are asked to cover for them. Take it.

C) Still other Overtime is available during high peek times.

1) Hospitals during emergencies.

2) Retail stores during Holidays.

3) Security companies almost always have Overtime.

While Overtime is a great time to make extra money, don't over do it. If you've worked too many extra hours let your supervisor know that you have to decline because you need the rest. Remember, your health is the most important thing.

And on the same subject, you should not be working two full time jobs at the same time.

The exhaustion could make you and others unsafe in both jobs.

You may think you can do it, but your body may have different plans. It may chose to simply shut down.

All of the Overtime you make is simply icing on the cake. It should be growing your Savings.

I remind you again. You are learning how to "Spend". So, the amount you put in your Checking should not change.

Do not factor the Overtime into your Spending.

# Temptation

Now that you have money in your Checking and Savings you will be able to measure your progress.

Seeing your progress will ease some of your anxiety when those unexpected bills appear out of nowhere.

However, your biggest anxiety will come from temptation.

Since you have been broke for so long, the temptation to spend the money you have accumulated will be overwhelming. Fight it.

One way to fight back is by setting Goals.

# Goals

Goals are like floors, you reach them one step at a time.

Imagine each step toward your Goal is a month.

Each floor is a year.

Your Plan is to reach the top, where your biggest Goal lies.

Your vehicle is you.

And, this Plan is the Map that you will use on your journey.

**There is a Chinese Proverb that says:**

The journey of a thousand miles, begins with a single step.

You have now taken the first step.

# Now let's see what this would look like in practice

Let's say you find a job.

I will use even numbers to make it easier to illustrate:

Your regular pay is $20 an hour.

Your Overtime pay is $30 an hour.

Your Double Time pay is $40 an hour.

In this job you get paid for 40 hours each week.

You get paid every Thursday.

Every week you get paid $800.

After taxes it comes to $647.22.

# Pay Days

Not all months have the same number of Pay Days.

Some have four and some have five.

1) January (4)          7) July (4)

2) February (4)         8) August (4)

3) March (5)            9) September (5)

4) April (4)            10) October (4)

5) May (4)              11) November (4)

6) June (5)             12) December (5)

In months with four pay days your monthly pay would come to $2,588.88 after taxes.

In months with five pay days your monthly pay would come to $3,236.10 after taxes.

If a paid holiday falls in your work week and you work it, you would be paid at the rate of time and a half for that day.

Your earnings for that week and month will be more.

# Let's Review

A) Weekly salary

    $800.00 Before taxes

    $647.22 After taxes

B) Weekly salary with Holidays

    $880.00 Before taxes

    $705.34 After taxes

C) Again, monthly salaries will depend on the number of Pay Days in that month.

1) January (4)          7) July (4)

2) February (4)          8) August ((4)

3) March (5)          9) September (5)

4) April (4)          10) October (4)

5) May (4)          11) November (4)

6) June (5)          12) December (5)

The Monthly salary will also depend on whether you work on a Paid Holiday.

1) New Years Day      January 1

2) Memorial Day      Last Monday of May

3) Independence Day  July 4th

4) Labor Day         First Monday in September

5) Thanksgiving      Fourth Thursday in November

6) Christmas Day     December 25th

C) Monthly earnings without working the Paid Holidays.

   Four Pay Days

$3,200.00 Before taxes

$2,588.88 After taxes

   Five Pay Days

$4,000.00 Before taxes

$3,236.10 After taxes

D) Monthly earnings after working a Paid Holidays

Four Pay Days

$3,280.00 Before taxes

$2,647.00 After taxes

Five Pay Days

$4,080.00 Before taxes

$3,294.22 After taxes

# Checking

Now let's assume that we've decided to transfer $1,800 every month to our Checking. This is the sum of our Permanent and Flexible bills. It is also less than the 70% of our monthly income after taxes.

Remember, the amount you transfer to your Checking does not change whether there are four or five Pay Days in a month.

## Savings

Your Savings will grow naturally when you have five Pay Days in a month.

Your Savings will also grow if you work any of the Paid Holidays.

It will grow even more if you are asked to work extra time or during peek times like emergencies.

# Illustration

Now, to illustrate this I am going to show you what this would look like if you did not work the Paid Holidays (Option A) and if you worked the Paid Holidays (Option B).

**Option A** (Without working Paid Holidays)

Four Pay Days: $2,588.88 After taxes.

Five Pay Days: $3,236.10 After taxes.

**Option B** (Working Paid Holidays)

Four Pay Days: $2,647.00 After taxes.

Five Pay Days: $3,294.22 After taxes.

# Option A

| Month | Income | Savings | Checking |
|-------|--------|---------|----------|
| January (4) | $2,588.88 | $788.88 | $1,800 |
| February (4) | $2,588.88 | $788.88 | $1,800 |
| March (5) | $3,236.10 | $1,436.10 | $1,800 |
| April (4) | $2,588.88 | $788.88 | $1,800 |
| May (4) | $2,588.88 | $788.88 | $1,800 |
| June (5) | $3,236.10 | $1,436.10 | $1,800 |
| July (4) | $2,588.88 | $788.88 | $1,800 |
| August (4) | $2,588.88 | $788.88 | $1,800 |
| September (5) | $3,236.10 | $1,436.10 | $1,800 |
| October (4) | $2,588.88 | $788.88 | $1,800 |
| November (4) | $2,588.88 | $788.88 | $1,800 |
| December (5) | $3,236.10 | $1,436.10 | $1,800 |

# Option B

| Month | Income | Savings | Checking |
|---|---|---|---|
| January (4)* | $2,647.00 | $847.00 | $1,800.00 |
| February (4) | $2,588.88 | $788.88 | $1,800.00 |
| March (5) | $3,236.10 | $1,436.10 | $1,800.00 |
| April (4) | $2,588.88 | $788.88 | $1,800.00 |
| May (4)* | $2,647.00 | $847.00 | $1,800.00 |
| June (5) | $3,236.10 | $1,436.10 | $1,800.00 |
| July (4)* | $2,647.00 | $847.00 | $1,800.00 |
| August (4) | $2,588.88 | $788.88 | $1,800.00 |
| September (5)* | $3,294.22 | $1,494.22 | $1,800.00 |
| October (4) | $2,588.88 | $788.88 | $1,800.00 |
| November (4)* | $2,647.00 | $847.00 | $1,800.00 |
| December (5)* | $3,294.22 | $1,494.22 | $1,800.00 |

CARLOS H. VASQUEZ

*Paid Holidays

Now that we've learned how much of your monthly earnings are going into your Savings, and how much is going into your Checking for you to Spend, let's look at how your Savings will grow.

Remember, any money you save in your Checking one month will roll over into the next month giving you more money to Spend. That should make you happy.

# Option A

**January is your first step in your Journey to Wealth and Prosperity.**

| Month | Income | Savings |
|---|---|---|
| December | $3,236.10 | $12,055.44 |
| November | $2,588.88 | $10,619.34 |
| October | $2,588.88 | $9,830.46 |
| September | $3,23610 | $9,041.58 |
| August | $2,588.88 | $7,605.45 |
| July | $2,588.88 | $6,816.60 |

You're half way there. Don't give up now. Look at the Progress you're making.

| Month | Income | Savings |
|---|---|---|
| June | $3,236.10 | $6,27.72 |
| May | $2,588.88 | $4,591.62 |
| April | $2,588.88 | $3,802.74 |
| March | $3,3236.10 | $3,013.86 |

| February | $2,588.88 | $1,577.76 |
|----------|-----------|-----------|
| January  | $2,588.88 | $788.88   |

This does not include other forms of Overtime or benefits.

I worked in one hotel that served breakfast, lunch and dinner for free to employees.

I don't have to tell you how quickly I paid off three maxed out Credit Cards and still had enough money in my Savings for any unforeseen expenses.

Now let's look at Option B.

# Option B

**Here too your first step is January, but in this Journey you work all the Holidays.**

| Month | Income | Savings |
|-------|--------|---------|
| December* | $3,294.22 | $12,404.00 |
| November* | $2,647.00 | $10,909.94 |
| October | $2,588.88 | $10,062.94 |
| September* | $3,294.22 | $9,274.06 |
| August | $2,588.88 | $7,779.84 |

The Paid Holidays are a great way to expand your Savings without changing your routine. Each step makes you even wealthier.

| | | |
|-------|--------|---------|
| July* | $2,647.00 | $6,990.96 |
| June | $3,236.10 | $6,143.96 |
| May* | $2,647.00 | $4,707.86 |
| April | $2,588.88 | $3,860.86 |

CARLOS H. VASQUEZ

| March | $3,236.10 | $3,071.98 |
|-------|-----------|-----------|
| February | $2,588.88 | $1,635.88 |
| January* | $2,647.00 | $847.00 |

*Paid Holidays

There are people who don't like to work the Paid Holidays. If you could work it for them, do so. Their lost is your gain.

This Journey only takes you from the ground floor to the first floor. Imagine starting the next year without Credit Card debt and with money in your Savings.

Now let's examine what you do when you have extra money in your Checking.

# Extra money in your Checking

If you spend all of your life working to Save, the one thing you won't save is your sanity. So, what I do with my extra money is have a little fun with it.

Let's review:

Any Overtime, in any Form goes straight into your Savings. You are getting richer.

Any savings you make by Spending wisely rolls into the next month. Giving you more money to Spend.

1) Spending wisely is the key. I can only show you what I do when I have extra money to Spend:

Occasionally, I take someone out to dinner without feeling discomfort about spending too much.

Another thing I do is buy Lottery tickets using a system that allows me to be responsible.

Here is how I do it:

There are five Lottery drawings per week.

I Spend five dollars in each drawing using different combinations.

a) One Mega ($2.00) + one Power ball ($2.00) + one Fantasy 5 ($1.00).

b) One Mega ($2.00) + one Power ball ($2.00) + one Super lotto ($1.00).

c) One Power ball (or Mega) + three Fantasy 5 (or three Super lotto).

The idea is to play responsibly by not playing more than $5.00.

Once in a while, when I have extra money, I buy a $10, $20 or $30 Scratcher.

Remember, the idea is to control the gambling. Don't let the gambling control you.

**Play Responsibly or Not at All!**

2) Another way I use the extra money in my Checking is to even out my Savings.

This allows me to see my progress more clearly.

Every month I look at my Savings. If I could make it even by transferring some of my extra money in Checking I do so.

By even I mean bringing the sum to the nearest $100, $500 or $1,000.

I will now show you how that works.

# Option A: Evening the months

| | Savings | Transferring from Checking |
|---|---|---|
| January | $788.88<br>$800.00 | $11.12 |
| February | $1,588.50<br>$1,600.00 | $11.50 |
| March | $3,036.10<br>$3,100.00 | $63.90 |
| April | $3,888.88<br>$4,000.00 | $111.12 |
| May | $4,788.88<br>$5,000.00 | $211.12 |
| June | $6,436.10<br>$6,500.00 | $63.90 |
| July | $7,288.88<br>$7,500.00 | $211.12 |
| August | $8,288.88<br>$8,500.00 | $211.21 |

CARLOS H. VASQUEZ

| | | |
|---|---|---|
| September | $9,936.10 | $63.90 |
| | $10,000.00 | |
| October | $10,788.88 | $211.12 |
| | $11,000.00 | |
| November | $11,788,88 | $211.12 |
| | $12,000.00 | |
| December | $13,436.10 | $63.90 |
| | $13,500.00 | |

# Option B: Evening the months

|  | Savings | Transfer from Checking |
|---|---|---|
| January | $847.00<br>$1,000.00 | $153.00 |
| February | $1,788.88<br>$2,000.00 | $211.12 |
| March | $3,436.10<br>$3,500.00 | $63.90 |
| April | $4,288.88<br>$4,500.00 | $211.12 |
| May | $5,347.00<br>$5,500.00 | $153.00 |
| June | $6,936.10<br>$7,000.00 | $63.90 |
| July | $7,847.00<br>$8,000.00 | $153.00 |
| August | $8,788.88<br>$9,000.00 | $211.12 |

CARLOS H. VASQUEZ

| September | $10,494.22 | $5.78 |
| | $10,500.00 | |
| October | $11,288.88 | $211.12 |
| | $11,500.00 | |
| November | $12,347.00 | $153.00 |
| | $12,500.00 | |
| December | $13,994.22 | $5.78 |
| | $14,000.00 | |

Evening the Saving amounts allow you to see the progress more clearly.

As you begin the following year with this amount in your Savings you will have the confidence to reach for your highest aspirations.

# Conclusion

Now that I have given you the Plan, I want to leave you with a few pieces of wisdom that I have gathered throughout my many years.

Remember, that even I don't know everything. But, I have learned a few things in my life and hope that these things can help you too.

# Couples

## Do Not! Do Not! Do Not!

Do not include your significant others Money in your budget. Remember, you and only you are learning how to spend.

I have heard of stories of women in their 30's who have never signed a check or balanced a check book.

As children this was left to their fathers. As teenagers to their boyfriends. And, as adults to their husbands.

If you are going to follow this Plan, set up your own Plan and let your significant other set up their own.

If you have a joint account, then sit down together and discuss how you can divide the Permanent and Flexible bills, and how much will be placed in each of your hands to Spend. The key here is discussion.

One way might be to have one person pay the mortgage, while the other pays the gas and electricity.

If you want to include the children, they can pay the Cable and/or the phone bill.

I remind you again. You make these Plans by sitting together.

Do not make these Plans without talking to each other.

Do not make Plans with money that belongs to someone else.

Remember, each person is learning how to "Spend".

# The Money in the Jar

Do not give your child a Credit Card!!!!!!!!!

Today it's a Credit Card, Tomorrow it's the National Debt. He won't know how to pay that off either.

This is how you teach him:

As a child give him an allowance of one dollar. But, do not give him paper money. Give him four quarters.

Set up a Piggy bank and a glass jar.

Every week when you give him a dollar in quarters, he has to put three quarters in the Piggy Bank and one in the glass jar.

He can only spend what is in the glass jar.

Every month what is in the Piggy Bank gets deposited into his very own Savings Account.

When he wants to buy something he knows that he has to think about how much money he has in the glass jar. He also has to consider how badly he needs what he wants to buy.

Today, he will learn the meaning of the Glass Jar and learn how to manage it.

Tomorrow, he may become a Congressman and he'll know how to manage The National Debt.

CARLOS H. VASQUEZ

# Kids

When I was in elementary school teachers were required to teach us how to manage money. We were taken on field trips to a local bank where we opened bank accounts. In Junior High School we had a similar class.

However, today kids do not get those classes. So, it's up to the parents to educate their children.

One way to do it is by setting up two Piggy banks; one labeled Savings and the other labeled Checking.

Every time someone gives them money, teach them to put some in the Checking and the rest in the Savings. By allowing them to spend the same amount from the Checking every week, they will learn to spend wisely.

The more they control their Spending, the more money they will have to spend.

Every month you can take them to the bank where they will be able to deposit their Savings into their own account. Give them a bonus by making their savings even.

# Hitting the Lottery

I can't give you much advice on what to do if you win a big Lottery. After all, I haven't hit one myself, yet.

All I can tell you is what I would do. Only foolish people say "I know exactly what to do if I hit the big one."

Since most of us are working people chances are that most of us know very little to nothing about getting rich, let alone about being wealthy.

Therefore, what I would do is take the payments. Never the lump sum.

Payments allows us to make mistakes and learn from them.

Even if you lose all your money foolishly this year, you have another check coming next year, and that one is bigger.

If you take the lump sum you will immediately lose half of it and pay taxes on the half you receive.

Once it's gone, it's gone. You will never get it back. What ever mistakes you make are permanent.

And, don't let anybody tell you they have a sure thing, if only you can give them money.

The only sure thing is death and taxes. Everything else is a maybe.

If it was such a "sure thing" they'd be rich.

CARLOS H. VASQUEZ

The only sure thing is that if they lose it, it won't be their money they lose, it will be yours.

I created this Plan for the average person. But, if you hit the big one, and you take the payments, you will be able to tailor it to your new found wealth.

Remember, that the amount is not what is important, the Plan is.

Follow the Plan

# Finally

I realize that there are people that have trouble thinking in long terms, such as months or years.

My advice to them is simply think in smaller terms, such as Pay Check to Pay Check.

Remember, that the amount that goes into your Checking should not change month to month. It should stay the same no matter how many Pay Days are in that month.

Let me illustrate this by keeping the transfer to Checking the same, at $1,800.

There are four months that have four Pay Days without Paid Holidays

    1) February     3) August

    2) April       4) October

**In these months you make $800.00 a week before taxes.
And, $647.22 after taxes.**

| Pay Day | Earnings | Savings | Checking |
|---------|----------|---------|----------|
| First | $647.22 | $197.22 | $450.00 |
| Second | $647.22 | $197.22 | $450.00 |

| Third | $647.22 | $197.22 | $450.00 |
|---|---|---|---|
| Fourth | $647.22 | $197.22 | $450.00 |
| Totals: | | $788.88 | $1,800 |

There are two months that have five Pay Days without Paid Holidays.

5) March     6) June

| First | $647.22 | $197.22 | $450.00 |
|---|---|---|---|
| Second | $647.22 | $197.22 | $450.00 |
| Third | $647.22 | $197.22 | $450.00 |
| Fourth | $647.22 | $197.22 | $450.00 |
| Fifth | $647.22 | $647.22 | No Transfer |
| Totals | | $1,436.10 | $1,800 |

There are Four months that have four Pay Days and one Paid Holiday.

7) January     9) July

8) May     10) November

We will illustrate what happens with just one of those months.

**January**

| First | $705.34 | $255.34 | $450.00 |
|---|---|---|---|

| Second | $647.22 | $197.22 | $450.00 |

| Third | $647.22 | $197.22 | $450.00 |

| Fourth | $647.22 | $197.22 | $450.00 |

There are two months with five Pay Days and one Paid Holiday.

    11) September   12) December

I will now illustrate what happens with just one of those months.

**December**

| First | $705.34 | $255.34 | $450.00 |

**This Paid Holiday is from Thanksgiving of the month of November.**

| Second | $647.22 | $197.22 | $450.00 |

| Third | $647.22 | $197.22 | $450.00 |

| Fourth | $647.22 | $197.22 | $450.00 |

| Fifth | $647.22 | $197.22 | No Transferring |

**Christmas falls in this month but will appear in the January Check.**

       Totals    $1,044.22  $1,800.00

# I end with this

It is easy to look back and judge yourself. And worst, let those feelings stop you from trying this Plan. Don't let it. Give it a chance.

Remember: Today is the first day of the rest of your life. Make it count.

Yesterday is gone. You can't bring it back. Only today and tomorrow is what counts.

Don't let others make you feel guilty about the past.

Forgive. Forget. And, move on.

We are all flawed human beings. None of us walk on water.

I am most proud, not of the things I've done, but of the things I could have done, and didn't.

Stay true to yourself and follow the Plan.

**Remember:**

It's Not About How Much Money You Make In Life.

It's About How Much Money You Keep

**And also, Remember This:**

There is no such thing as a handicap.

There is only an inconvenience.

An inconvenience only becomes a handicap,

When you stop trying.

So, Good Luck!

# Other Kernels of Wisdom

Every time you reach a goal, set your goals higher.

If your goal is to save $5,000 and you reach it, don't spend it.

Set a new goal of $10,000.

When you reach that, set a new goal of $15,000.

If your goal is to get a high school diploma, and you reach that.

Set a new goal to get an Associate degree.

If you reach that, set a new goal to get a Bachelors degree.

## AND

If you don't know where you are going, remember the old saying:

**When you don't know where you're going. Any road will take you there.**

It means you have to take a road!

## Remember:

Time waits for no man or woman. Don't waste it.

It is never too late.

I could of.

I should of.

I would have.

**Is not an option.**

**JUST FOLLOW THE PLAN**

CARLOS H. VASQUEZ

# I Quit Money

I can't count the number of jobs I've had where I've asked myself: "What the hell am I doing here?"

Jobs where the pay was low, management was racist or I wasn't appreciated and/or respected.

Jobs where I strongly long to say the words "I Quit!".

But, I stayed. Why? Because I had no "I Quit" money.

"I Quit" money is the amount of money you have in your savings account that allows you to quit that miserable job. Money that will sustain you for at least two years while you search for a better opportunity.

By sustain, I mean be able to pay all your bills including rent or mortgage, gas, electricity, car payment and food.

You notice I left out credit cards. Pay those off and get rid of them once and for all. At 28% they are stealing from you.

By opportunity I mean a place where you work that will recognize your value and reward you in both pay and benefits.

A place which will see and recognize your past, present and future contributions to the company.

A job is not an opportunity. A job is simply a gas station where you fill up on the way to an opportunity.

If you have read this book fully you will have learned that the problem is not saving money.

The problem lies in learning how to spend.

You have also learned that if you have a job that is paying you through Direct Deposit, the money should be going to your Savings Account, not your Checking Account.

You also would have learned how to set goals. Remember, that goals are like flights of stairs, you reach them one step at a time.

Now let me show you where those flights of stairs should be leading you.

First, I want to remind you to never leave a job unless you have a definite source of income. I did that once. I left a job to finish school and landed up with neither.

The ultimate goal you should be reaching for is to save twice your yearly salary, before taxes, in your Savings Account.

You should also have all your credit cards paid off. Your car fully paid off if possible. Your car insurance fully paid each year. And, your student loan manageable if you can.

The less monthly payments you have the easier it is to reach your goals.

Let me illustrate:

If you make $30,000 a year, you should have at least $60,000 in your Savings Account.

I know that what I am saying sounds impossible. And, so did climbing Mount Everest, but now people climb it every day.

If you give The Plan I've laid out in this book a chance you'll see that it isn't as impossible as it appears to be. As you see your savings grow each pay check it will give you greater confidence.

Remember, that a journey of a thousand miles begins with a single step.

Put one foot in front of the other and begin that journey.

# How to cure the student loan problem.

When you attend an institution of higher learning, the school makes you an implicit promise that you will make more money with their degree.

If you graduate with an Associate degree you should not be making less than $40 thousand dollars a year.

If you graduate with a Bachelor's degree you should not be making less than $60 thousand dollars a year.

A Master's degree should be getting you at least $80 thousand dollars a year.

A Phd, nothing less than a six figure income.

The Universities want to say they don't make any such promises. However, that is because they get paid up front.

But, what if they were the co-signers instead of your parents.

They would have to make sure that upon graduation you would have reached those levels of income before you started picking up the repayment of your student loans.

Here is how it would work:

Thirty days after graduation re-payments would begin.

If you had not reached those levels of income, the Universities would have to begin making the re-payments for you until you reached that level of income.

Upon reaching those levels of income you would pick up the payments, however, you would not be responsible for any of the payments already made by the Universities.

They would certainly have an incentive to assure you a better job upon graduation or a greater incentive to make their tuition more affordable.

# Have you figured out a Plan?

**You can use this as a guide:**

1) **First**, your Plan must be your Plan and your Plan only.

It must not include other people. Not your boyfriend. Not your friends. Not your family. Not strangers.

Your Plan must be yours and yours alone.

2) **Second,** you must sit with a pad and pencil and list what needs to be paid and how much income will be needed for daily expenses, such as food and gas.

3) **Third,** it must include a continuous source of income. Something predictable and constant, such as a job.

4) **Fourth,** it must provide for a constant building of a safety net, such as a Savings account. That is only touched in dire emergencies.

5) **Fifth,** and this one should be known by everyone buying Real Estate:

You must not create any new expenses such as credit cards or unnecessary purchases.

**Good Luck with "Your New Plan".**

Remember this:

Life without a Plan is like driving without a steering wheel.

You may hope that the car gets you where you want to go, but eventually you are only headed to a collision.

With a Plan, like with a steering wheel, you can steer from lane to lane around life's difficulties and eventually reach your destination.

Printed in the United States
by Baker & Taylor Publisher Services